# Doodlebops™

# Friends and Favorites

## Coloring and Activity Book

## Kids' Favorite Rockin' Band!

### www.doodlebops.com

© Disney

COOKIE JAR™

kids'CBC

The Canadian Broadcasting Corporation™

**DOODLEBOPS™ and COOKIE JAR™ & © 2007 Cookie Jar Entertainment Inc.**
**Used under license by Carson-Dellosa Publishing Co., Inc.**

ISBN 978-1-60095-256-2

# Would you like to meet the Doodlebops and their friends?

2

## "I'm Deedee Doodle!"

3

"I'm Rooney Doodle!"

01475 Friends and Favorites

# "I'm Moe Doodle!"

5

## "We're the Doodlebops!"

# Color by letter to find the hidden picture.

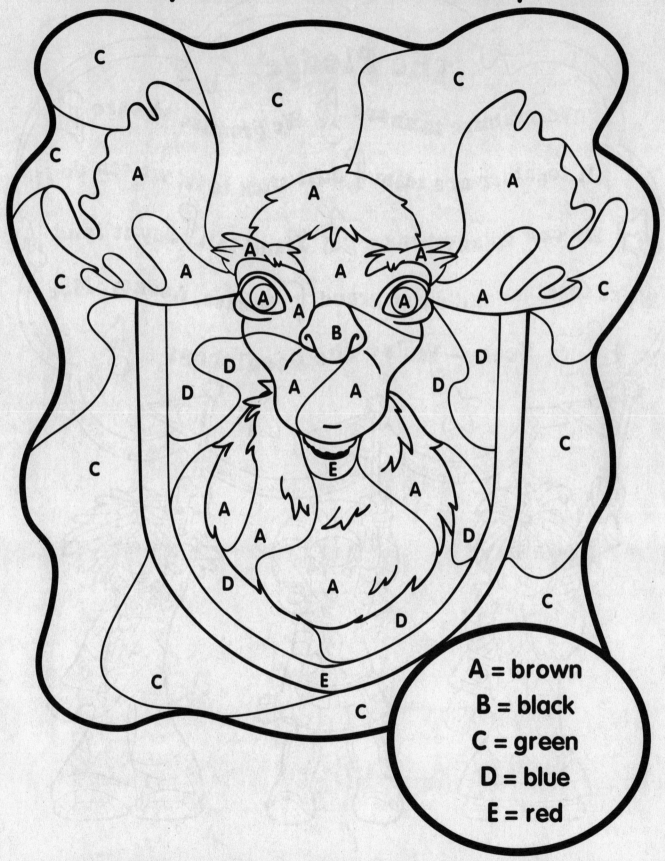

A = brown
B = black
C = green
D = blue
E = red

## Mr. Moosehead says, "The Doodlebops are just dandy!"

# Can you say the Doodlebops Pledge with us?

8

cut

# Make your own Doodlebops Pledge flag.

1. Cut out the flag.
2. Attach the flag to a stick or ruler with tape.
3. Say the pledge.

## Say it loud; say it proud!

Mr. Moosehead says, "I hereby pledge to always listen to the pledge!"

# It's Jazzmin!

# Name the pictures in each row.
## Circle the pictures in each row that rhyme with the first picture.

## Jazzmin likes to rhyme.

# Connect the dots 1-10. Start at the ⭐.

# Fix Jazzmin with scissors and some tape.

cut

cut

**The Doodlebops' friend, Jazzmin, is all mixed up! Her head is on her waist.**

# Draw a picture of yourself with Jazzmin.

**Who is pink, purple, bouncy, and fun?**
**Deedee Doodle!**

 01475 Friends and Favorites

# Color all of the things on this page that are pink.

## Deedee's favorite color is pink.

**Deedee loves to dance. Dance, Deedee!**

20

# Circle all of the things that begin with the letter D.

## D is for Deedee.

**Queen Deedee**

Deedee is thinking about her favorite snacks.
Do you know what they are?

01475 Friends and Favorites

**Deedee likes to tell Mudge knock-knock jokes.**

# Count the floating bubbles.

## Mudge is busy taking a bath.

# How is Mudge feeling today?

01475 Friends and Favorites

glad

sad

mad

surprised

angry

happy

## The look on your face can show how you feel.
## A happy face is the best face of all!

**Who is tall and always asking questions?**
**Rooney Doodle!**

# Color all of the things on this page that are blue.

## Rooney's favorite color is blue.

**Rock on, Rooney!**

# Draw the path the egg will take to get to the nest.

## Rooney is good at inventing things.

01475 Friends and Favorites

# Circle all of the things that begin with the letter R.

## R is for Rooney.

01475 Friends and Favorites

**Rooney performs the Wobbly Whoopsy.**

01475 Friends and Favorites

# Draw a line from Rooney to his favorite snacks.

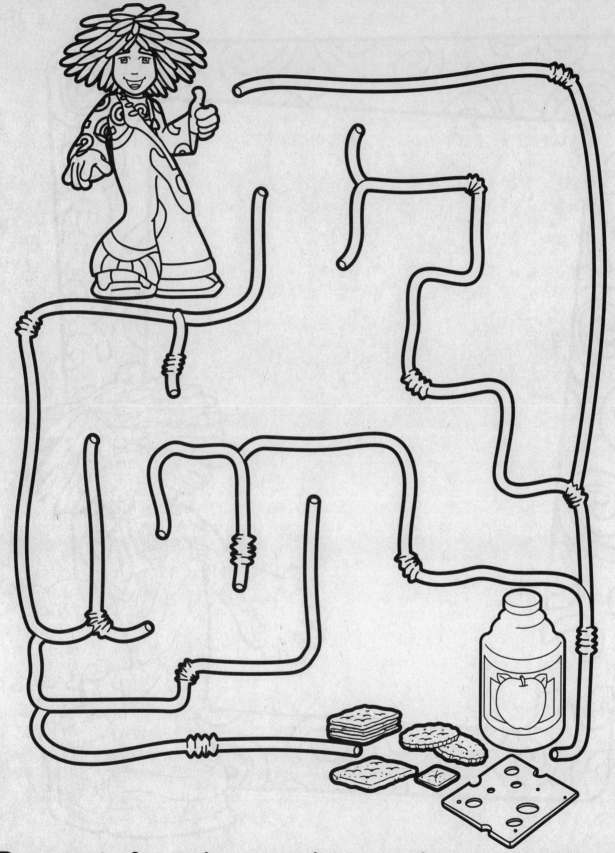

## Rooney's favorite snacks are cheese, crackers, and apple juice.

01475 Friends and Favorites

# Draw a picture from your favorite book.

## Rooney likes to read.

# Color and cut out the bookmarks.
# Use them when you read your favorite books.
# Color and cut out the book labels.
# Use them to label your favorite books.

cut

**36**

**Audio Murphy says, "Howdy, Doodles!"**

37

**The Doodlebops film a video while Rooney plays his invention, the Honk-a-Phone!**

**Deedee shows Audio Murphy some dance moves for the Ding Dong Doodle Dance-Off.**

# Follow the steps to dance the Zebra Shuffle with Deedee.

1. Start here
2.
3.
4.

Z is for Zebra.

01475 Friends and Favorites

# Follow the lines to count 1-10.

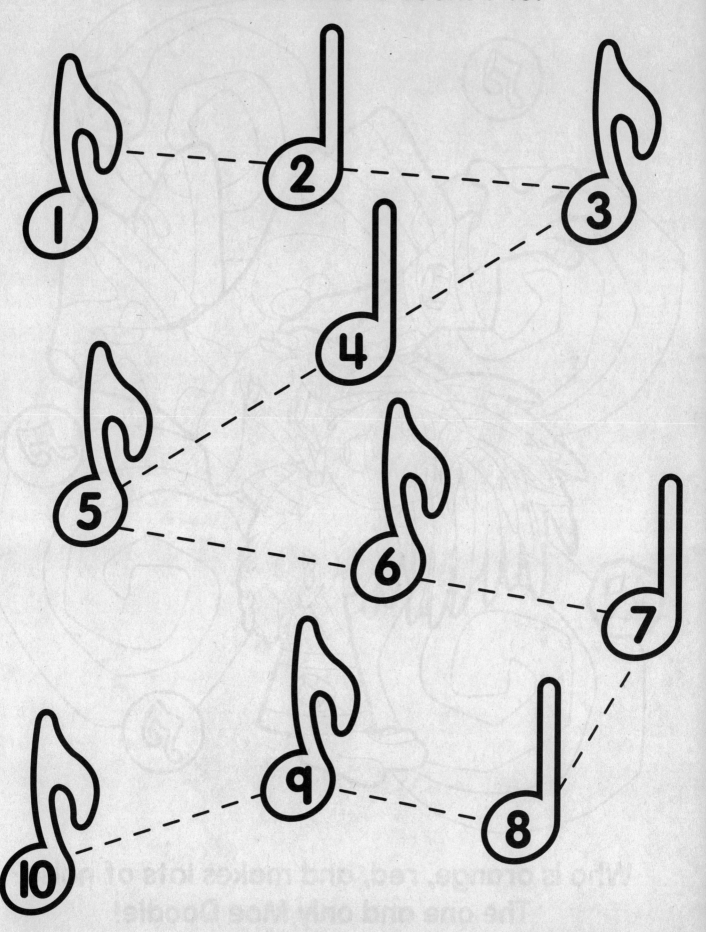

**Who is orange, red, and makes lots of noise?
The one and only Moe Doodle!**

# Crash! Crash!

01475 Friends and Favorites

# Color all of the things on this page that are orange.

## Moe's favorite color is orange.

# Circle Moe with orange.

## The Wig Heads ask, "Where's Moe?"

 01475 Friends and Favorites

# Circle all of the things that begin with the letter M.

## M is for Moe.

# When Moe isn't hiding, he likes to pull the rope!

47

**"Refreshing!"**

# To find out what Moe's favorite snacks are, connect the dots 1-10. Start at the ⭐.

# Draw and color a picture of your favorite snacks.

01475 Friends and Favorites

# Circle Deedee's favorite snacks with pink.
# Circle Rooney's favorite snacks with blue.
# Circle Moe's favorite snacks with orange.

# Honk! Honk!

01475 Friends and Favorites

**The Doodlebops love to get on the bus.**

# Connect the dots 1-10. Start at the ⭐.

## Get on the bus!

## It's Bus Driver Bob!

01475 Friends and Favorites

**"Hey, come on! We're gonna take a bus ride!"**

01475 Friends and Favorites

# Draw a line to help Bus Driver Bob find the Doodlebops.

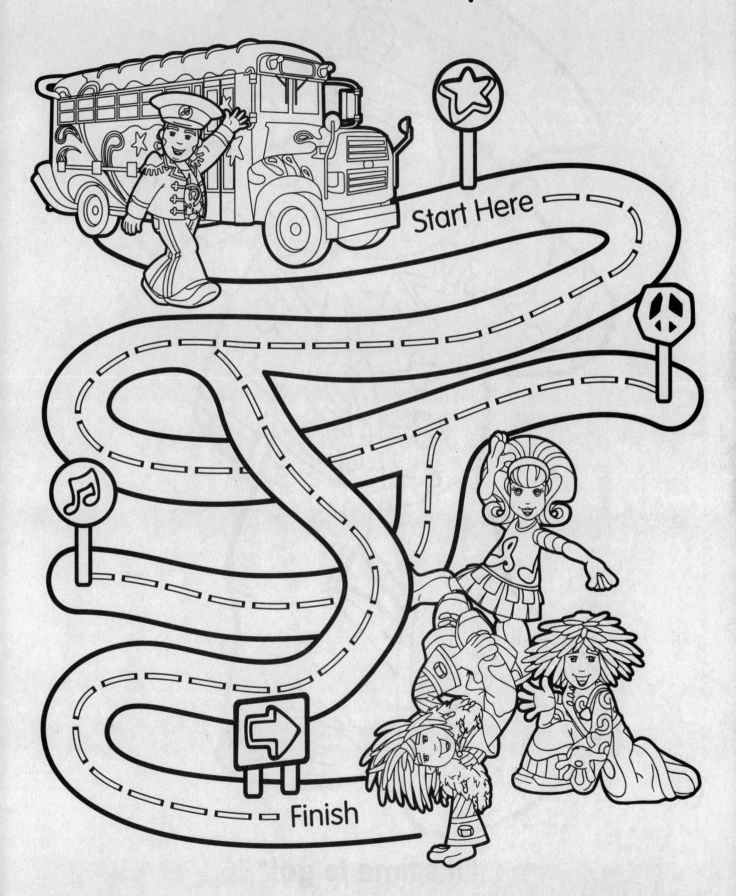

Start Here

Finish

**"It's time to go!"**

# Circle all of the things that begin with the letter B.

## B is for Bob.

# Connect the dots 1-14. Start at the ⭐.

**Bus Driver Bob gets the Doodlebops to their shows on time so that they can play music for all of their fans!**

# Color the buses to match the color words on the crayons.

red

green

purple

yellow

orange

blue

01475 Friends and Favorites

# Circle the differences in the pictures.

# Cut out the pieces and put them together.

cut

# Draw a picture of yourself with Bus Driver Bob.

# Help Jazzmin and the Doodlebops find Mudge and Audio Murphy.

# The Doodlebops and their friends are playing hide-and-seek.

# Color star 1 orange. Color star 2 blue. Color star 3 pink. Color star 4 green. Color star 5 purple. Color star 6 red.

**The Doodlebops love to sing and dance!**

You go, girl!

01475 Friends and Favorites

# Color the largest heart red.
# Color the smallest heart pink.

**Deedee loves to play her keyboard.**

# Use the key to color the objects.

**Rooney rocks on his guitar.**

# Connect the dots 1-10. Start at the ⭐.

01475 Friends and Favorites

# Draw a line to help Rooney find his guitar.

01475 Friends and Favorites

# Color each guitar to match the color word.

**Playing the drums is fun.**

01475 Friends and Favorites

## Moe is always on the move.

# Where's Moe?

01475 Friends and Favorites

## Time to play!

80

# Circle the shadow that matches Moe.

01475 Friends and Favorites

# Circle the hidden objects.

## "Don't pull the rope!"

01475 Friends and Favorites

# Draw a line to help Moe find his drums.

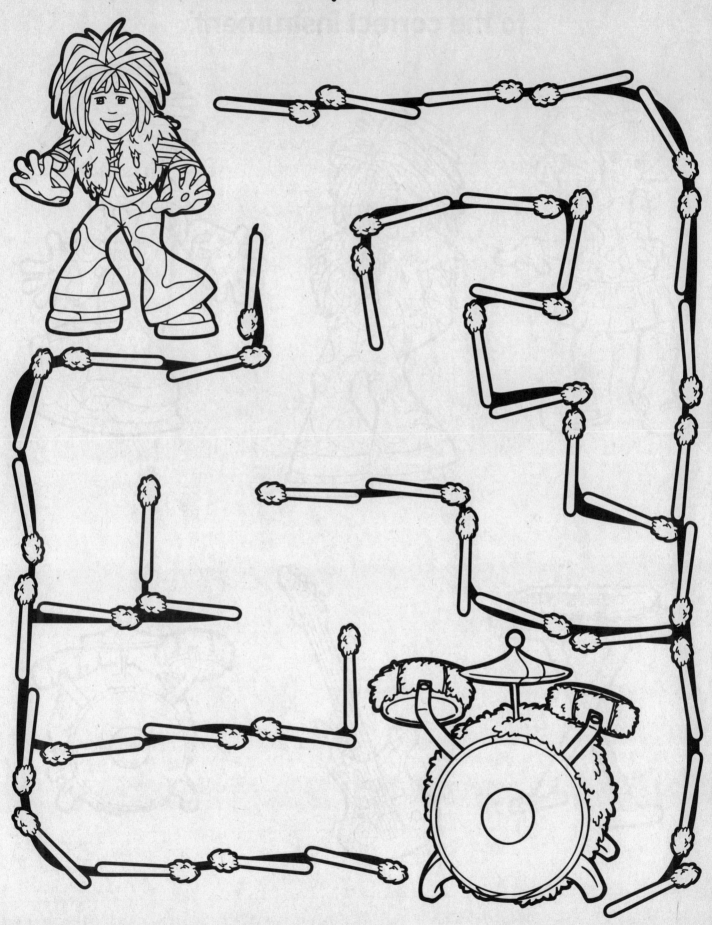

83

# Draw a line to match each Doodlebop to the correct instrument.

# Circle Deedee's instrument with pink.
# Circle Rooney's instrument with blue.
# Circle Moe's instrument with orange.

# Draw lines to match the pictures that are the same.

# Draw a picture of yourself with your friends.

 01475 Friends and Favorites

# Circle the Doodlebops' favorite things hidden in the picture.

Doodlebops' Favorites

My name is _____.

My favorite Doodlebop is _____.

Circle your favorite Doodlebop.

My favorite color is _____.

Color the crayon with your favorite color. CRAYON

My favorite food is _____.

My favorite drink is _____.

Circle the Doodlebops' favorite snacks that you ♡ best.

GRAPE JUICE     MILK     APPLE JUICE

I ♡ the Doodlebops™ because _____

_____

_____.

# Draw lines to match the objects that are the same.

# Play tic-tac-toe with a friend.

# Circle everything that the Doodlebops will need for the concert.

"When we get together, we're always having fun!
We're the Doodlebops!"

# Color and cut out the puppets below. Then, cut out the puppets and stage from the back cover. Use the puppets and the stage to create your own Doodlebops adventures.

cut

cut

cut

cut

01475 Friends and Favorites